THE

Temperance Battle not Man's but God's.

WRITTEN AND PUBLISHED

FOR THE

Instruction and Encouragement

OF

THE FRIENDS OF TEMPERANCE

THROUGHOUT THE UNITED STATES,

BY REV. JOHN MARSH, D.D.,

COR. SEC'Y OF THE AM. TEMP. UNION.

"The battle is not yours but GOD'S."—2 CHRON. xx. 15.

New-York:

AMERICAN TEMPERANCE UNION, No. 10 PARK BANK.

1858.

To the Friends of Temperance.

If the thought here presented shall impress, encourage and animate your hearts, as it has my own in our arduous conflict, I shall be abundantly rewarded for the labor of drawing it out, and sending it to you. May we hear the voice of Him who says to us, "Be of good courage and play the man for yourselves and for the cities of our God."

J. M.

J. P. PRALL, PRINTER BY STEAM, SPRUCE-ST., N. Y.

THE TEMPERANCE BATTLE.

"The battle is not yours but God's."—2 Chronicles xx. 16.

There was something fearful in that voice when Moses stood in the gate of the camp, and said, Who is on the Lord's side? let him come unto me. Rebellion had broken out. The people had said to Aaron, "Up, make us gods which shall go before us; for, as for this Moses, the man that brought us up out of the land of Egypt, we wot not what has become of him. And when Moses came down from the mount, and Joshua heard the noise of the people as they shouted, he said unto Moses, There is a noise of war in the camp. But Moses said, It is not the voice of them that shout for mastery, neither is it the voice of them that cry for being overcome, but the noise of them that sing do I hear." It was indeed the noise of revelry and mirth, and yet it was the noise of war; of war against heaven; and God, in his anger, ordered a separation of the precious from the vile; and there fell of the people that day, about three thousand men. But there are other conflicts besides those in which God directly takes vengeance on his enemies—conflicts between his people and their foes—which, from some peculiar circumstances, are often pre-eminently God's. When the children of Ammon and Moab, and Mount Sier, came against Judah, from beyond the sea, Jehosaphat feared, and set himself to seek the Lord, and proclaimed a fast throughout all Judah; and they cried mightily unto the Lord for deliverance. Then upon Jehaziel, the son of Zechariah, came the Spirit of the Lord; and he said, Hearken ye, all Judah, and ye inhabitants of Jerusalem, and thou King Jehosaphat, thus saith the Lórd unto you, "Be not afraid nor dismayed by reason of this great multitude ; for the battle is not yours but God's." Theirs it was primarily and actively. They were to fight and conquer, or die. But theirs it was not alone. Theirs it was not in all its great and ultimate bearings. Higher interests than theirs were at stake, even the interests of God and his universal government. Therefore, said the Lord by the prophet, " Be not afraid nor dismayed by reason of this great multitude ; for the battle is not yours but God's."

This most impressive truth admits of an application to all spiritual and moral conflicts—to conflicts with Atheism, and idolatry, with error, and oppression, and iniquity of every description ; but I shall improve it, as I most justly may, in relation to that great conflict with INTEMPERANCE, which, for the last thirty years, has been engaging, and is now engaging, the hearts and hands of thousands and millions. To all such, in antagonism to this great evil, I would say, THE BATTLE IS NOT YOURS BUT GOD'S.

And yet, that I may not be misapprehended, and that none may be lulled into inaction, I would first observe, Yours most rightly and properly it is. Yours, as bound to take care of your own bodies and souls, and keep them from the arts of the great destroyer ;—yours, as fathers and mothers, set to protect and rescue your children from the fangs of the monster ;—yours, as philanthropists called to have compassion on the weak and the suffering, to make sacrifices for the good of others, and to pull the victims of the cup out of the burning ;—yours, as patriots and citizens, who are to protect the community in which you live from corruption, violence, and crime ; from heart-rending cruelties, and awful catastrophes ;—yours, as Christians, endowed with the higher power of divine wisdom and influence to emancipate the church and reform the world. In a word, yours it is as living in an age when the ravages of intemperance are most deeply felt, and when it can be expelled only by your agency and instrumentality ;—yours, for God has made it such and will hold you responsible for the most vigorous and exterminating warfare. And yet, it is not yours. This is a paradox which the men of this world will not understand, and of which, perhaps, many of you are utterly ignorant. When you go forth in your own strength, or take to yourselves the glory of your achievement, it is manifest that you are. It is only when men go out of themselves, and look above, and around, and contemplate the vast interests in which they are concerned, and reflect on that INFINITE ONE with whose glory is connected, for good or for evil, all the actions of mortals, that they learn that human interests are as nothing, and that the great movements of men for the blessedness of the world, are not theirs, but God's.

Does the fool say in his heart, THERE IS NO GOD?—Does he affirm that all the glorious mechanism of the Universe, from the sun that rolls in the heavens to the finest filament of an insect's wing, comes from the fortuitous concourse of atoms, and that man is without a moral governor or guide? The men of God may resist him for his folly, and for the rescue of their own faith and hope; but the battle is not theirs, but God's. And so if millions on millions of benighted Pagans bow down to gods of wood and stone; and missionaries of the cross, in love and compassion, leave father, and mother, and houses, and lands, and go forth to contend with inhuman rites and horrid superstitions, and perhaps lay down their lives in the conflict, the battle is not theirs, but God's. And if truth is banished from among men, and error, dark and damning, sits brooding over the nations, or walks abroad as an angel of light; and men, enlightened from above, stand forth the exponents and defenders of stern realities, the battle is not theirs, but God's; for he is the God of truth, and no lie may be permitted in his vast dominions. And so, from every stand-point you can take, whether as individuals, as parents, teachers, philanthropists, patriots, Christians, the temperance battle is yours;—but so much higher interests are involved, that yours are lost or swallowed up in them. THE BATTLE IS NOT YOURS BUT GOD'S.

Do you ask for the proof? It requires no proof. I should as soon think of offering proof that God exists, or that he is possessed of the attributes of God. It must be so. It cannot be otherwise. To say that God is the friend and not the enemy of Intemperance, or that he is in any way indifferent to this great conflict, would be the greatest of absurdities; not to say, blasphemy itself.

Such an evil—so destructive to man's best interests for time and eternity—so mocking God in his exquisite workmanship of the human frame, turning it into a bloated, staggering, loathsome thing, and bringing it by thousands and millions to a dishonored grave—so wasting God's property, food enough to feed an empire, and treasure enough in fifty years to fill the world with Bibles, and ministers, and churches—so at war with the Bible, and the Sabbath, and the Spirit—engendering pollution, blasphemy, contention, violence, suicides, murders—blasting revivals, polluting churches, degrading ministers at the altar, going before the missionary of the cross to the heathen and making them ten-fold more inacessible and more the children of hell than before—such an evil, pervading the high and the low, the rich and the poor, entering the councils of nations, and the temples of Jehovah—never ceasing, never ending, no stop in the circuit of those horrid wheels which mangle and crush human bodies without number, and no cessation in its more dark and terrific work of ruin to the soul—a work which "has sent into perdition more men and women than that deluge which swept over the highest hill tops, engulfing a world, in which eight only were saved"—such an evil, a voluntary outbreak of the wicked heart against all the physical and moral laws of his kingdom, God must hate and oppose, or he could not be God.

The drunkenness of Noah, and Lot, and Dathan, and Abiram, and Nabal, and Ephraim, and Benhadab, and Belshazzar, with his royal guests, drinking wine out of the stolen vessels of the Lord, were the abhorrence of his soul. Warning after warning did he give his people against this body and soul destroying sin, with all its causes and accompaniments. "Woe unto them that rise up early in the morning, that they may follow strong drink, till wine inflame them." "While they are drunken as drunkards, they shall be devoured as stubble fully dry." All the accessories of drunkenness—fashion, custom, hospitality, gain—no matter what they may be—are, with him, participants in guilt. "Woe unto him that giveth his neighbor drink; that puttest thy bottle to him, and makest him drunken also. Drink thou also. The cup of the Lord's right hand shall be turned unto thee, and shameful spewing shall be on thy glory." Against the traffic, causing drunkenness, robbing the poor when it catches him in its net, hear the thunder of his wrath: "Woe to him that coveteth an evil covetousness to his house, that he may set his nest on high; that he (being rich) may be delivered from the power of evil. Thou hast consulted shame to thy house by cutting off many people, and hast sinned against thy soul. For the stone shall cry out of the wall, and the beam out of the timber shall answer it. Woe to him that buildeth a town with blood, and establisheth a city by iniquity."

Intemperance contests God's right to everything which he has made; to the body, with all its wonderful workmanship; to the mind, his own bright image; to the heart, made to love and fear him; to the immortal soul, which Christ hath purchased with his own blood; to the Sabbath, as God's day, set apart for his glory; to the fruits and grains which he has prepared for man, for beast, and for the fowls of heaven; to the earth itself, as his rest, where "he will dwell with men, and they shall be his people, and God himself shall be with them, and be their God, and where God shall wipe away all tears from their eyes." Such a time as millennium, Intemperance says, shall never come. I will destroy the beautiful body, and send it to an untimely grave; I will dethrone reason; I will take away the heart; I will break up family peace and domestic happiness; I will extract from the grains and the fruits of heaven a drink which shall turn man into a fiend, and earth into a field of blood; I will make the Sabbath the day of my triumphs; will snatch souls from the arms of Jesus Christ and turn them into hell. Earth, with all its promised blessings of peace and boundless joy, shall be the everlasting abode of drunkenness, madness, despair, and death. Is it any wonder that the battle should be God's battle?

His providence has ever shown with an awful emphasis that it is his battle. His providence is his law, in its results —not always visible at first—sometimes full of mystery. Distillers, and brewers, and importers, and venders often roll in wealth and luxury, which they have gained in the slaughter of thousands. "Pride compasseth them about as a chain. Violence covereth them as a garment. They are not in trouble, as other men are; neither are they plagued like other men. Their eyes stand out with fatness, and they have more than heart could wish. They set their mouth against the heavens, and their tongue walketh through the earth." God's people contemplate them with wonder, and "waters of a full cup are wrung out to them." But the end is not to-day, nor to-morrow.

Follow them to the death-bed scene. Read their history ; the history of their sons ; the history of their estates. Into what snares does God often suffer them to fall ! If not drunkards themselves, cursed with drunken sons, or by daughters torn, and scathed, and peeled by drunken husbands ; or perhaps themselves harrassed, reproached, tormented by the victims of their cup, living, dying, or gone to judgment. Enter that once magnificent and beautiful dwelling. There was once all that could make life desirable ; wealth, beauty, intelligence, love ; but the wine cup was there. It was the pride of the house. Rich stores were in the cellar. Guests flocked thither to become participants in the joy. Warning and admonition were given. "Who hath woe? who hath sorrow? who hath wounds? who hath redness of eyes? They that tarry long at the wine," was sounded in their ears. But they heeded not. They drank, they laughed, they mocked. But the poison did its work. The husband and father went down to the grave, an idiot sot. One son after another died a drunkard ; and poverty and contempt were the portion of the more innocent ones. Of how many a family it has been the history, none can tell.

Every poor-house, every mad-house, every penitentiary, and house of correction, filled with the degraded and the ruined, is the stamp of the Almighty upon this vice and its inhuman traffic. Neighborhoods, and States, and Kingdoms that have given their strength to the manufacture and sale of intoxicating drinks, and who have said, "By this craft we have our wealth," have been cursed in all their borders with poverty and crime. Look at France, with its millions of acres devoted to the culture of the vine ; look at England, Scotland, and Ireland, with their mammoth distilleries and breweries, destroying breadstuffs enough to feed millions a day ; look, too, at our own country, where have been poured forth rivers of the fiery poison, and how has the curse everywhere prevailed! "With what measure you mete, it shall be measured to you again." "They that sow to the wind, shall reap the whirlwind." Sixty thousand drunkards in Great Britain and forty thousand in America form an annual procession to the grave, and the mourners go about the streets in rags, and shame, and woe. The distiller has rolled up wealth, but God has not suffered him to enjoy it. The importer and vender have rolled up wealth, but God has not suffered them to enjoy it. They have howled upon their beds in anguish and in fear of an hereafter. Every license given has brought a curse upon the State. Broils and murders have been fearfully engendered. Around the dram shop have risen an ungodly generation, to lie, and curse ; to defraud, and blaspheme ; to despise the Sabbath, and prepare for hell. A drunken son has brought a distiller's grey hairs with sorrow to the grave ; and a drunken wife has lain in the bosom of the vender, only to tear out his heart-strings. Terrible have been the dealings of Providence in this warfare, as whole families, father, mother, sons, and daughters have filled drunkards' graves ; and as a nation or a State, licensing the curse, has been deprived of the brightest of its youth, and the noblest of its statesmen.

If we have need of further illustration of the truth that the battle is God's battle, we have it in the wonderful success which in the last twenty years, has attended it. Not with more contempt did Goliath look down upon David with his sling and stone, than did the army of distillers and brewers, of venders and consumers, upon the feeble band which commenced the conflict. Even men of enlarged minds and sober thought, viewed it as a hopeless effort to change the habits of a nation, to save the drunkard and break up the richest traffic. But behold the result! A nation born in a day : not by might, nor by power, but by weapons from God's armory, light and truth, stripping off the damning delusion, and unveiling and bringing to light the horrors of the traffic. Farms, factories, workshops, ship-yards, social circles, the habitations of the moral and religious, thousands and tens of thousands who travel on the land and the sea, redeemed from the temptation and the curse ; the church and the ministry relieved from their worst foe. The very drunkards of the land, given up in despair, at one period by thousands and tens of thousands, burst their chains, and sprung into liberty. And distant nations have mingled in the triumphs. It has been all of God, who hath here marvelously "chosen the foolish things of the world to confound the wise, and the weak things of the world, to confound the things which are mighty, and base things of the world, and things which are despised, to bring to nought things that are," that men may know that it is his work.

And when the advocates and professed supporters of the cause have, at any time, forgotten or forsaken God, and refused to recognize him in prayer and in any of their efforts, they have at once most signally failed. Neither God nor his people would sustain them. Every successful movement in this great conflict, from its commencement to the present hour, has shown that it is not man's work, but God's. What hath God wrought! has been the exclamation of every reflecting mind. And every defeat has come not from God's power, but from the combinations and designs of wicked men. And is it any wonder, I again ask, that it is God's battle? Intemperance is the great enemy of God and his Son. God must oppose it and will oppose it, though earth and hell are arrayed for its support. You may be on the Lord's side, and help on the mighty conflict but THE BATTLE IS NOT YOURS BUT GOD'S.

And now I desire to lead you to some improvement of this subject, and to make some suitable reflections.

And first, if the battle is not yours but God's, then, as those engaged in it, you have no reason to be ashamed. Many would feel ashamed of being engaged in this great conflict. They could not endure the jeer of the luxurious and refined; the proud man's contumely; the scorn of the delicate lady; rejection from the wine party and the social circle. Polished families have denied that they had any sympathy with the movement. Ministers, in rich congregations, have shrunk from naming it in the pulpit; and men who have gloried in being recognized as presidents and directors of large and rich philanthropic institutions, have refused all enrolment in this war. But to whom belongs shame—to those who are with God, or to those who are against him? To whom belongs shame—to those who are arresting and turning back the tide of sorrow and woe, and saving souls from death, or to men and women who add fuel to the fire, which destroys the fairest works of God? Oh thou bleeding Lamb of God! who didst humble thyself and become obedient unto death, even the death of the cross, despising the shame, forgive us that we have ever blushed when battling in thy cause; or that we have not counted it our highest glory to gather up the lowest outcasts, chosen of thee to be jewels in thy crown.

2. If the battle is not yours but God's, then you may leave all your adversaries to settle their controversies with him.

Many complain of you as interfering with their business, their habits, and their pleasures. May we not, say they, do as we will with our own ; are we not our own masters ; may we not eat, and drink, and buy, and sell as we please ? All interference is unwarranted and insulting. This is a land of liberty and of protection of rights, and who are ye to judge us ? But it is not you that interfere and judge, but God. He makes war upon them—their business, their habits, their pleasures. He says, " Wo unto them that rise up early that they may follow strong drink, till wine inflame them." He says, " Woe unto him that putteth the bottle to his neighbor's lips, and makest him drunken ;" and while you pity them in their delusion and do all you can to save them and their offspring, you may leave them to settle all their controversies with him. The battle is not yours but God's.

3. If the battle is not yours but God's, then be not dismayed by reason of a great multitude of foes, nor fearful of final results.

What if these foes are mighty ; what if interests opposed are vast, reproaches deep, and passions violent ; what if kings and rulers, and judges, and all the powers of darkness are allied against you ; who is this great Leviathan that you should fear ? What if he has millions of treasure at his control, and his fortresses and strongholds are without number ; and what if he cuts down forty thousand victims year by year ; " Hearken ye, all Judah and ye inhabitants of Jerusalem, and thou king Jehosaphat, Thus saith the Lord unto you, Be not afraid nor discouraged by reason of this great multitude, for the battle is not yours but God's." We measure not our swords with this terrible foe alone. God is with us. We are fighting his battle. All the great principles of his physical and moral government sustain us. He is the protector of the weak, the helper of the suffering. He enlightens the minds, and moves the compas-passion, and bows the wills of men. He thwarts the counsels of enemies ; and makes all the engines of evil, the very manufactories of drunkenness, the distilleries and drinking houses of the land, plead powerfully for their own destruction. Every rum murder has a tongue more eloquent than man. Every drunkard, dying of his delirium tremens, crying out before his time, "The fires of hell are in my bosom; I am surrounded by serpents and devils damned; I am lost, lost, for ever lost!" strikes terror into the hearts of the people. The old nations, Egypt, and Greece, and Rome, had no power to overthrow vice. Their very religion was baptized in pollution, and priest and philosopher loved it; so that, in the midst of their intelligence and splendor they sank in their corruption and miserably perished. But we have the gospel—a mighty lever, by which God lifts up the nations. That fills the soul with an abhorrence of the wrong; with pity for the suffering; with a spirit of self-sacrifice for the good of others; and a zeal for conquest which can never be subdued. Through this great power, the power of the cross, united to the authority of his law, and the terrors of his providence, and a judgment to come, God Almighty will conquer. It cannot be that this world, on which he has set his affection, for which Christ died, should forever be given up to this vile sin; that God's sabbath shall forever be desecrated by this unholy traffic; that men made for honor, glory, and immortality, shall forever be thus dragged down through drunkenness to perdition.

Let the unbelieving, and the faint-hearted, and those who cringe before the violence of wicked men, say, it is impossible. Who is unmindful of the past? Who can forget that great wave of mercy which rolled over the Emerald Isle in the days of Father Mathew? Who, that mighty movement which, in 1840–1, stirred every fibre of love and compassion, bearing thousands and tens of thousands of miserable inebriates to the Home of the free? Every city, town, and village was then moved. Fathers brought their sons, wives their husbands, sisters their brothers, to sign the pledge. Platoon after platoon, rough and ragged, pressed on for deliverance.

> "They came like the winds, when forests are rended;
> They came like the waves, when navies are stranded."
> "Their wives and children standing by,
> Sent forth the shout of victory."

Another is coming. I see it in the distance. The preparation is plain. I know not what holds it back. Ten thousand slain from under the altar cry, "Oh, Lord, how long?" But it will be a tornado of wrath. When God shall let loose the winds, and the people shall rise in mass and demand the extinction of the traffic, it will be done. The very distillers and venders will cry to the rocks and the mountains to fall on them, and hide them from an indignant world. Legislatures will everywhere be as ready to enact prohibitory laws, as they now are to license the accursed traffic ; and as universal will be their enforcement, as is that of the laws against counterfeiting or murder. Men may not believe it. But who can limit the Almighty ? Who can comprehend his power to enlighten the minds and sway the hearts of men ? If God be for us, whom should we fear ? Who, successfully, can be against us ?

4. If the battle is not yours but God's, then it may reasonably be expected that all the professed people of God will be foremost in the fight.

They are his soldiers ; enlisted to fight his battles, and all his battles. They may not choose some, and neglect others. They may not say, " Here, in the name of our God, will we set up our banners," but there will we stand neutral. If the battle with Intemperance is God's battle, then he has a right here to the service of every Christian ; to the service of every minister ; to the service of every pulpit ; and to the service of every Christian press. None may excuse themselves from the conflict, saying, Temperance is not religion ; it is a mere dietetic or sanitary concern ; a secular and political conflict ; it concerns the outer, and not the inner man ; the body, and not the soul ; it belongs to the week-day, and not to the Sabbath ; to the public hall, and not to the consecrated sanctuary. None may stand aloof because the battle may be directed by wicked men who know not God, and acknowledge neither his authority nor his providence ; nor because it is conducted in a manner inconsistent with Christian character and at variance with Christian taste. Nor may any plead that they have higher interests at stake, or that this will bring them into conflict with men whose wealth is needed for the support of the church. IT IS GOD'S BATTLE, and God will hold them to it and to its right direction.

" If," said that great and noble warrior who first stormed the battlements of Alcohol, Dr. Justin Edwards, " if Satan can cause it to be believed that this is a mere secular concern, and those who manufacture, sell, and use the weapons of his warfare not hear of their sins on the Sabbath, when God speaks to the conscience; or be entreated from the pulpit, his mercy-seat, by the tears and blood of a Saviour to flee from coming damnation, the adversary will keep possession of his stronghold. Church members will garrison it, and provision it, and fight for him. From the communion table, he will muster recruits, and find officers in those who distribute the elements, to fight his battles, perpetuate his warfare, and people, with increasing numbers, his dark domains to the end of time. If we may not, in this warfare, fight on the Lord's day, when he himself goes forth to the battle, and commands in the field ;—if we may not use his weapons forged in heaven, and, from the high places of his erection, pour them down, thick, heavy, and hot upon the enemy, we may fight till we die, and he will esteem our iron as straw, and our brass as rotten wood ; our darts he will count as stubble, and laugh at the glittering of our spear. There is no coping with this enemy, but with weapons of heavenly temper, from the armory of Jehovah, on the day when he goes forth, and creation, at his command, stands still to witness the conflict. Then it is as conscience, kindled from above, blazes and thunders in the heart of the enemy, that he is consumed by the breath of the Almighty, and destroyed by the brightness of his coming."

But why should we thus speak, when such momentous interests are at stake? What opponent is there like Intemperance to the conviction and conversion of sinners, and the speedy establishment of Christ's kingdom among men? What so desecrates the Sabbath, vitiates youth, causes men to flout at God, and Christ, and Heaven, hinders missions, and turns souls by thousands into hell? Enter the habitation of the drunkard ; and, in half an hour, you may witness a violation of every commandment of the decalogue. He abjures God, is an idolater, a blasphemer, disobedient to parents, a murderer of himself and his children, Oh, how obscene! a thief, a slanderer, a coveter of what others possess, and, worse than an infidel, makes no provision for his own. Does his Heavenly Father say to him, in infinite compassion, "My son, give me thine heart," the lost wretch cries, "Give me rum." Does the blessed Saviour stand knocking at his door; he, angry at his importunity, cries out, "Away with him; crucify him!" Does the Spirit of grace, finding him poor, and blind, and naked, and destitute, and in want of all things, whisper to his soul, "Repent, and have heaven?" he rushes to the drink, that, in the Lethean waters, he may drown all reflection. And with five hundred thousand such in our land, going down to death, has the Church no interest in this battle? With intemperance standing in the way of the progress of Christianity around the world and the glories of millennium, has the Church nothing to do in this matter? May the ministry hold their peace; aye, drink with the drunken, and countenance, by their presence, the Bacchanalian festival, and be innocent? Oh, that terrible malediction! let it be feared, "Curse ye Meroz; curse ye bitterly; for they came not to the help of the Lord, to the help of the Lord against the mighty." But we are called not so much to warn or to chide, as to bless. From our American Zion have gone forth our noblest warriors. The names of Beecher, and Hewitt, and Edwards, and Humphrey, and hundreds of others will go down to posterity with sweetest fragrance. Our churches have been our strongholds when everything else has fallen. And every Home missionary, and every missionary in the foreign field, has been a valiant soldier in the outskirts of the camp where the enemy has early entrenched himself, or commenced dragging the poor Pagans by millions to the pit. For this we bless our God. So let Zion be valiant, and the world will be saved.

5. If the battle with Intemperance is God's battle, then prohibition and not license of the traffic, its great source, is the true principle of legislation.

Civil government is an ordinance of God, established for his glory, and for the good of men. Rulers stand in the place of God. "By me kings reign, and princes decree justice." And that they may meet their high responsibilities, they need be men of self-denial and self-control. "It is not," said the wise man, "for kings to drink wine, nor for princes strong drink, lest they drink and forget the law, and pervert the judgment of any of the afflicted." And in all acts of legislation they must be on the Lord's side—resisting all evil, protecting the people from evil doers, and sustaining the principles of God's moral government.

In all his conflicts with evil, the Governor of the Universe never gives license ;—no, not for an hour. It is always PROHIBITION, PROHIBITION. "Thou shalt do no murder. Thou shalt not steal. Thou shalt not bear false witness." To license an evil doer, is to protect the criminal and not the victim. The licensed vender selling poison to his weak brother and bringing him to the drunkard's grave, is the criminal protected by the State ; and the cries of the broken-hearted victim and his beggared family will go up, and not in vain, into the ears of the Lord of Sabaoth.

Political expediency, a belief that a little gained is better than nothing, and the demands of men who cry, "By this craft we have our wealth," may plead for some compromise with the traffic ; but with the entire license system, God's warriors can have no fellowship. It may hold out the promise of regulating an acknowledged evil, but it upholds and honors that evil. It takes away responsibility and a sense of guilt. All its accompanying pledges of prohibition on election and other days, are idle. It commissions death with hell following, to go forth and kill and destroy ; and it will be the wonder of coming generations that a Christian Legislature should ever enact a license law, and that a Christian governor should ever give it his sanction. The mere selfish total abstainer who declaims against law, says, I will destroy the traffic by withholding my patronage ; while there the fortress stands, scattering arrows, firebrands, and death. What cares the enemy for his patronage, while he can entice and make drunkards of his children! The abstinence of four millions of abstainers from the grogshops, does but little to diminish their number. The extreme moral suasionist says, Moral suasion will do the work, and the distiller and vender must be reasoned out of their business. What care they for his reasoning? Nothing ; while he discards and casts contempt on civil government, the greatest and most glorious ordinance of God for the peace, the order, and redemption of the world.

Law there is in heaven, and law there must be on earth ; but law based on the eternal principles of right. Nothing may be allowed by a human government which is not by the divine ; having love for its basis, and a principle of love vitalizing every department. "Love worketh no ill to his neighbor ; therefore love is the fulfilling of the law." And hence, actuated, as we believe and trust, by this noble principle, and seeking protection for the people, in answer to their demands, our Legislatures have cast aside License and enacted Prohibition. They have met with storms of wrath, from all who would uphold Intemperance; from all who would make money on the ruin of their fellow-men; from all who drink wine in bowls, and care not for the affliction of Joseph; from all who would make political capital out of the debased appetites and passions of the community; and their action has even been overthrown, as conflicting, not with the eternal principles of right, but with legal technicalities or constitutions of State. But in such legislation, they have been on God's side; and God's helpers in the great battle. And whom have they to fear? Or of what should they be ashamed? Oh, I love to remember the outburst of a noble patriot and Christian to the State that dared first of all take a stand for the right and overturn "the throne of iniquity, established by law." Let it forever adorn the pages of humanity. "PEOPLE OF MAINE. The God of heaven bless you for achieving such a victory. You have followed the most adroit conqueror the world has ever seen. You have steered for the capitol itself, with all its magazines and materiel of war. You combat with the body of death and sin itself. When mighty conquerors and crafty politicians will be forgotten, the laurels on your brows will be freshening and blooming with a beauty and glory which will be immortal." *

And in view of the blessed results of that legislation, its amazing diminution, almost instantaneously, of drunkenness, pauperism, madness, and crime, we say, Shame on any people who uphold not their government in it; who fail of causing such laws to be executed; who have a price put into their hands to get wisdom and redemption, but have no heart for it. Shame on a State which, having once extended protection to the victim, and proclaimed deliverance to ten thousand suffering families, reverses its acts, and goes back to the protection by license of the heartless criminal.

The progress of the right may be slow, but it is sure. An age of advance in all sciences and arts which meliorate the condi-

* Professor Moses Stuart.

tion of man, will not discard a principle of government that will do more to relieve the world of pauperism, violence, and crime, than all acts of regulation which have ever been adopted. The last may be first. Britain, though feeling that her immense revenue from the licensed traffic may be essential to her life, may be the first, under the instruction of God's truth, to throw it all to the winds, and adopt the right principle—the principle of prohibition. One of the first nobles of the nation has termed the liquor traffic "the cancer of the State, which must be cut out by the knife;" and when the good Queen shall ask, as she one day will, in the spirit of earnest inquiry, "Is it right to license a traffic which turns 600,000 of my subjects into brutes and fiends, and sends 60,000 annually to drunkards' graves," who can doubt what her answer will be? Be instructed, O States of America! God has a controversy with the desolating traffic; a controversy with every voter who, at the ballot-box sustains it; with every legislator who makes laws for its protection: with every magistrate and citizen who fails in his duty to proscribe and abolish it. "If ye be with him, he will be with you," and grant you a blessed deliverance in all your borders; but if ye fight against him, he will fight against you, and your land shall be a desolation and a curse.

6. If the battle is not yours but God's, then they who expect it will die with you will be greatly mistaken.

When those who cried out, "These men that have turned the world upside down have come hither also," expected, by their expulsion and death, to put an end to Christ and his kingdom, they were destined to disappointment. And so it has been with all the Neros, and Caligulas, and Charleses, and upholders of slavery and the traffic in intoxicating drinks. Once and again has the shout gone up from the enemy's camp, "The battle is over; the cause of temperance is dead." When the first pledge had done its work; and in the use of vinous and fermented drinks, moderate drinkers were satisfied, and reformed men went back by hundreds to ruin, the cry rang through the land, "The cause is dead; temperance is a failure." When that whirlwind of mercy, of which we have spoken, had purified all the low dens of drunkenness, and brought to their feet, by almost a miracle, an army of besotted men, and no more was, to human view, at once to be effected, again it was said, "The cause is dead." And when the Prohibitory Law of the State of New York was overthrown by that unparalleled decision of the Court of Appeals, three Judges dissenting, a shout of victory went up from every dramshop, tavern bar, and distillery, and from all the dark regions of the pit; and again we hear the echo around the world, the Maine Law is dead. But it is GOD'S BATTLE; and though it is in the hands of feeble men, and earth and hell are combined against it; though there is occasionally discomfiture and defeat, and good men grow weary, and warriors die in the field, yet God lives; and through all time God's Bible will proclaim a woe against drunkards and drunkard makers, and God's providence will be against all the men and women who shall uphold in the world this terrible evil. Rejoice not ye who contend with God in this matter. He is neither faint nor weary. Fear not ye who have done your duty, and are passing away. God will raise up another generation, who will be valiant in the fight. But it is for you to train them for the battle; to teach your children in the house and by the way, in the Sabbath school and day school, all the principles of this great conflict;—for you to bring them, as did the father of Hannibal his son to the altar, and cause them to swear eternal enmity to this great destroyer.

7. If the battle with intemperance is God's battle, then you ought to support it with your wealth.

The silver and the gold is the Lord's; made by him, and for his glory; but silver, gold, flocks, herds, fruit, grain, the magnificent mansion, stocks, securities, labor, skill, all that God has loaned to man for his comfort, Intemperance, where it rages, engulfs it all. Nothing is left to the poor drunkard of all that his Heavenly Father had given him. An hundred millions have been annually wasted in this land on intemperance; and when God has risen in his wrath and indignation, and his compassion too, and excited his friends to come to his help and battle this foe, no amount of money wanted in its defence has been withheld. Thousands on thousands have been subscribed to delude the people, defend the prosecuted vender, fee lawyers, bribe Legislators and Jurors, and perpetuate the curse. But on the other hand, how few have given liberally to aid God in the conflict! How few of our men of wealth (but here and there one) have made donations worthy of the cause! How many of large estates, and giving tens of thousands in their wills to other benevolent enterprises, have made no mention of this! And how few of the churches have ever embraced it in their annual collections, as having any connection with the great interests of God's kingdom. Not a tithe of the money saved to the temperance community by this cause, has ever been brought to its extension. And hence the battle has been conducted amid the greatest embarrassments. Lecturers have retired in want. The press has been stopped. Societies in debt have been disbanded. And only faith that God would, in some way, take care of his own, if man in his penuriousness did not, has upheld us in the conflict. The impression that temperance was a work of faith and labor of love, and needed little or no pecuniary aid, has been most delusive and destructive. While it has been peculiarly a work of the masses in the popular meeting, the great results, where money has been freely given and documents freely scattered, and truth perseveringly sustained, shows that, were means furnished in proportion to the greatness and importance of the conflict, we should soon see the monster evil tottering to its base, and wealth saved to the nation of which we have faint conceptions. Is penuriousness either wise or right in this matter? No, friends; come with your wealth to the help of the Lord against the mighty. An obligation rests upon you which you cannot throw off and be guiltless. Oh the folly of building vast jails, and poorhouses and asylums for the victims of the cup, and giving nothing to aid in delivering the land from the curse.

8. If the battle is not yours but God's, then you know to whom to look for aid;—to look in childlike, humble, fervent, effectual prayer. "The Lord of Hosts is with us; the God of Jacob is our refuge." And what is more, we know to whom to give all the glory of success. "Not unto us, not unto us, but to thy name, O Lord, be all the glory." But not to dwell on this, a theme for eternity,

I must close, beloved friends, with a rebuke and an exhortation. A rebuke. If the battle is not yours but God's, then how shameful, how wicked all lukewarmness and yielding up of this great conflict.

God, the mighty God, is moving heaven and earth to subdue this his greatest foe, and to save millions of souls from perdition. Interests are at stake of which a Newton or a Gabriel could have no conceptions. Earth is to be delivered from two-thirds of its poverty and insanity, its cruelties and casualties, and heaven to be filled with ransomed ones ; and yet, because of the labor and the cost, perhaps the ridicule, the reproach, we yield the conflict, and settle down in apathy and repose, almost forgetting that there is a foe to be vanquished. Oh, is this our zeal, our love, our gratitude ? Is this because the battle is not yours, but God's ? Will you throw it all upon him to finish it ? Will you weary God with a sluggishness which, in any worldly enterprise, would bring you to poverty and rags ? Oh, look at that rumseller or distiller in your very neighborhood, dragging perhaps your own sons down to death, and be humbled and confounded. Yes, look ; and take up, as you well may, the bitter lamentation of the venerable Cotton Mather, " O my soul, thy Maker and thy Saviour, so worthy of thy love, a Lord whose infinite goodness will follow all thou doest for him with remunerations beyond all conception glorious, how little, how little is it that thou doest for him ; at the same time look into thy neighborhood ; see there, a monster of wickedness will serve a master that will prove a destroyer to him, and whose wages will be death ; he studies how to serve the devil ; he is never weary of his drudgery ; he racks his invention to go through with it. Ah ! he shames me ; he shames me wonderfully. O, my God, I blush and am ashamed to lift up my face to thee, my God."

And yet you say, " It is vain to serve God. We have done all we can. All hands hang down. All hearts faint. Our enemy, once quailing, has again come forth, haughty, overbearing, cruel. His footsteps are deep in human gore ; while fashion, appetite, interest, and more than all, political craft and power, are leagued for his support." And what if it is all so ; and there are adverses and dark days, and, to you, humiliating triumphs ? THE BATTLE IS NOT YOURS BUT GOD'S. Opposition we should pity more than fear. Excuses and apologies men may make for worshipping in the temple of Bacchus ;—bow down to fashion and appetite they may ; roll up riches and gain political power they may ; mock at all the teachings of God's providence and the physical laws of their own nature they may ; drink wine in bowls with their offspring, and be drunken they may ; the battle is God's ; and "Wo to him that striveth with his Maker." When he cometh in his wrath and his fury, " they shall not drink wine with a song, strong drink shall be bitter to them that drink it." O ye wealthy families that are at ease in Zion, who drink wine in bowls and care not for the misery around you, God may bring you down wonderfully. A drunken husband and father here ; a vile and ruined son there ; a daughter, tender and greatly beloved, coming home scathed and peeled from the cruelties of a drunken partner. Laugh you may, and jeer you may, and despise all God's warnings and all the teachings of his providence you may, but who can compass the bitterness that may overtake you? But " in that day shall the Lord of Hosts be for a crown of glory and a diadem of beauty unto the residue of his people, and for strength to them that turn the battle to the gate."

Never, no never, friends, was there such encouragement in this conflict as to-day. God, even our God, has come down, not in his wrath, but in his mercy, to soften, and melt, and turn the hearts of this great nation to himself; to convince all evil-workers of their evil doings ; to convert, we will hope, the distiller and the brewer, the vender and the consumer of strong drinks from all their hostility to themselves, to Him, and to their fellow immortals hastening to eternity. Never, no never, has the sun shone upon our land when it presented such a spectacle of moral grandeur as it does to-day. The temperance cause has done much to prepare the way of the Lord ; and now that God has so wonderfully revived religion in the nation, surely the temperance cause must follow in its wake, and soon witness blessed triumphs. Up, then, Oh, ye temperance warriors! buckle on your armor afresh, and march forward to the speedy and glorious termination of your conflict.

1. Present yourselves a perfect example of entire abstinence from all intoxicating liquors as a beverage, in your persons, your families, your social pleasures, and in all the labors of life.

2. Warn every man, and exhort every man against all such use as tends to ruin. In whatever company or condition you are, meekly, but boldly and unflinchingly, give battle to those

drinking usages which have dragged thousands and tens of thousands to the pit.

3. Treat the traffic as the scourge of humanity; the great instrument of Satan in destroying the peace and happiness of the world, and sending souls without number to destruction.

4. Uphold and strengthen all legislation which shall protect the victim and not the criminal; which shall suppress and prohibit the temptation, and let the tempted go free; which shall be on God's side, and not on the side of the adversary.

5. Go through all your towns and villages, and pledge again every man, woman, and child, not to touch, taste, or give the accursed thing; and especially go down among the rising generation, and train them all to an abhorrence of the cup.

6. Sustain able lecturers in the field; scatter broadcast tracts and documents; and in all your organizations, and efforts be united, efficient, liberal, strong in faith, and of good courage. Look upward in every trial and under every difficulty. Be faithful to the end. This terrific scourge of earth shall be driven out. Help or no help from civil government, from politicians, from those who are at ease in Zion, it will be driven out. Do you ask for an assurance? You have it here, THE BATTLE IS NOT YOURS BUT GOD'S.

The true action of Civil Government.

ADDRESS OF HIS EXCELLENCY THE GOVERNOR OF NEW HAMPSHIRE AT THE OPENING OF THE LEGISLATURE IN 1857.

The Act for the suppression of Intemperance is having a salutary effect. It is more fully regarded and practically sustained than any License law ever had in the State. In many towns, the sale of intoxicating liquors is wholly abandoned, and in others, it is sold only, as other penal offences are committed, in secret. I am not aware that there is a city or town in the State where spirituous liquors are openly sold. That there are places where the law is secretly violated, is not doubted, and the same may be said of every law, whether statute or common, from the highest to the lowest grades of offence.

That the sale of spirituous liquors has greatly diminished since the Act took effect, is plainly visible; and this fact is freely conceded by most candid men, whether they approve of its objects and provisions or not. Those engaged in the illegal trade, dare not expose it openly, but sell it in the darkness of midnight. It is very evident to all, and it is next to an impossibility to be otherwise, that sales must be extremely limited in number and quantity where the traffic must be carried on in dark holes and loathsome dens, where men tremblingly feel their way, and where the light of day is not admitted to witness the transaction, or countenance the offence.

If there is to be any restraining law, any law to prevent unlimited sale, the present law is as mild and as liberal as an efficient law can be. The license system has ever proved, and everywhere proves, only a special privilege to a favored few—an unlimited sale by a licensed class, a legalized method of encouraging intemperance with all its train of acknowledged evils.

OF THE GOVERNOR OF VERMONT TO THE LEGISLATURE OF 1856.

My confidence in the power and duty of the Legislature to prohibit the traffic in intoxicating liquor as a beverage, remains unshaken. I deem the principle of Prohibition to be in perfect accordance with our Constitution, and in harmony with the obligations which the government owes to the people. Few if any, of the sources of evil have been so prolific of mischief, have sent forth so vast a desolation, and produced such overwhelming misery throughout all the departments of social and domestic life, as the sale of intoxicating liquors. The people have a right to demand at the hands of their agents, protection from the evil, so destructive of the happiness and well-being of society.

I conceive that the true interests of the State, and the hopes of the rising generation, require a Prohibitory law, with ample powers effectually to enforce its provisions, prescribing penalties commensurate with the offences it prohibits, and adapted to accomplish its great design, the extinguishment of the traffic. The constitutionality of several of the most important provisions of the present law of the State upon this subject, has been settled by the Supreme Court, a tribunal which has the just confidence of our citizens.

OF GOVERNOR WRIGHT OF INDIANA TO THE LEGISLATURE OF 1856.

Whatever difference of opinion may have been heretofore entertained on this subject, no man can shut his eyes to the fact that, through our State, numerous places have been opened, or established, for the unrestrained sale of spirituous liquors, in which the young and unwary have been decoyed to contract tastes and habits, which the resolves of a subsequent life cannot control; if they have not already entered upon the courses of dissipation and vice.

It is imperatively the duty of the Legislature, in the exercise of a wise discretion, to enact some constitutional law, in accordance with public sentiment, of sufficient stringency to restrain and suppress this growing evil.

www.ingramcontent.com/pod-product-compliance
Lightning Source LLC
LaVergne TN
LVHW011145110826
845150LV00008B/2524

* 9 7 8 1 4 1 8 1 9 2 1 7 4 *